PIANO • VOCAL • GUITAR

SONGS OF THE
1990s

🔊 **81 Songs with Online Audio Backing Tracks**

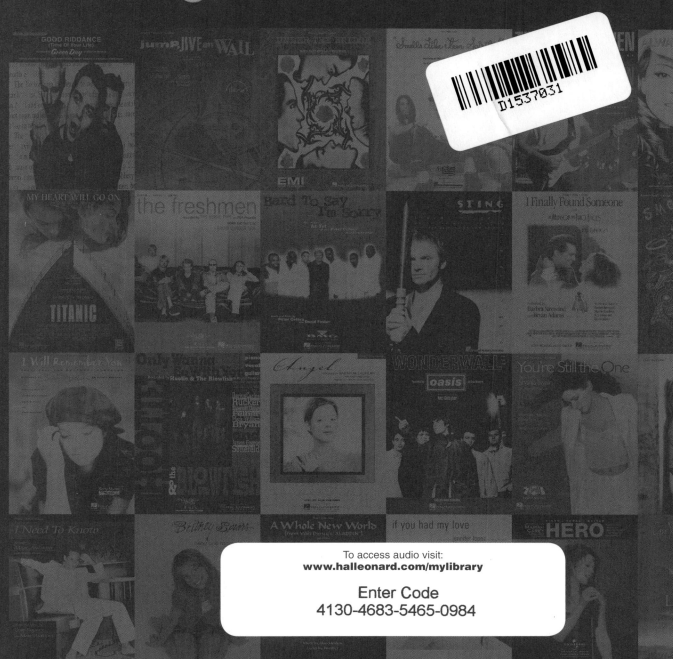

To access audio visit:
www.halleonard.com/mylibrary

Enter Code
4130-4683-5465-0984

ISBN 978-1-4950-0036-2

HAL•LEONARD®
CORPORATION
7777 W. BLUEMOUND RD. P.O. BOX 13819 MILWAUKEE, WI 53213

Visit Hal Leonard Online at
www.halleonard.com

ALWAYS BE MY BABY

Words and Music by MARIAH CAREY,
JERMAINE DUPRI and MANUEL SEAL

Lyrics (under staff):

We were as one, __ babe,   for a mo-ment in ____ time. __

I ain't gon-na cry, __ no,   and I won't beg you to ____ stay. __

And it seemed ev-er-last-ing, that you would al-ways be mine.
If you're de-ter-mined to leave, __ boy, I will not stand in your way. __

Now you want to be free, _____ so I'll let you fly, _____
But in-ev-i-ta-bly _____ you'll be back a-gain, _____

'cause I know in my heart, __ babe, our love will nev-er die. __
'cause you know in your heart, __ babe, our love will nev-er end. __

You'll al-ways be a part of me. __ I'm part of you in-def-i-nite-ly. __

Ooh, dar - ling, 'cause you'll al - ways be ___ my ba - by. I know that

you'll be back, boy, when your days and your nights get a lit - tle bit

cold - er. ___ I know that you'll be right back, ba - by.

Ba - by, be - lieve me, it's on - ly a mat - ter of time, time. ___

BECAUSE I LOVE YOU
(The Postman Song)

Words and Music by
WARREN ALLEN BROOKS

ANGEL

Words and Music by
SARAH McLACHLAN

AS LONG AS YOU LOVE ME

Words and Music by
MARTIN SANDBERG

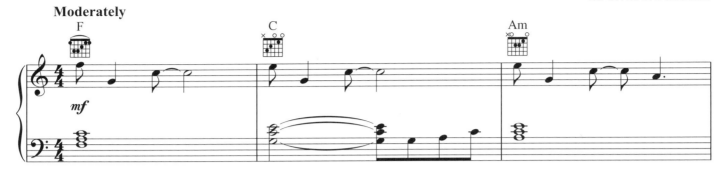

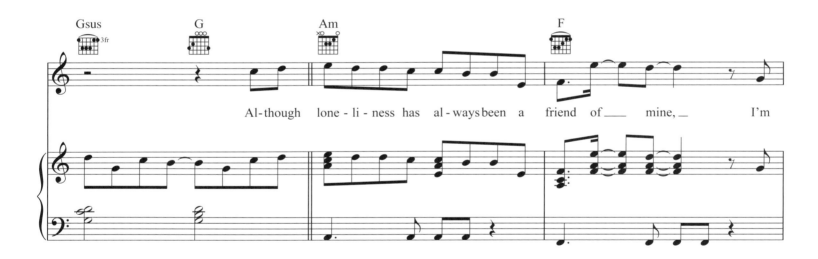

Al-though lone-li-ness has al-ways been a friend of ___ mine, ___ I'm

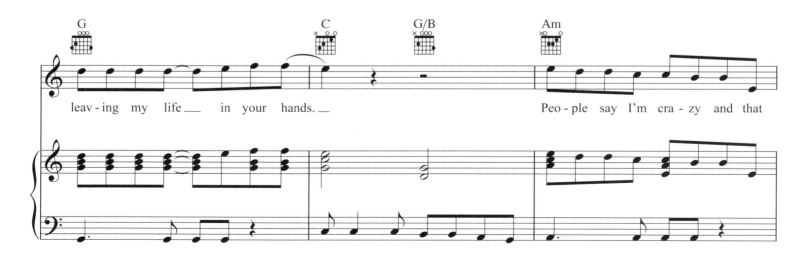

leav-ing my life ___ in your hands. ___ Peo-ple say I'm cra-zy and that

...BABY ONE MORE TIME

Words and Music by
MAX MARTIN

BARELY BREATHING

Words and Music by
DUNCAN SHEIK

BEAUTIFUL IN MY EYES

Words and Music by
JOSHUA KADISON

BELIEVE

Words and Music by BRIAN HIGGINS,
STUART McLENNEN, PAUL BARRY,
STEPHEN TORCH, MATT GRAY
and TIM POWELL

**Vocal written one octave higher than sung._

BLACK OR WHITE

Words and Music by
MICHAEL JACKSON

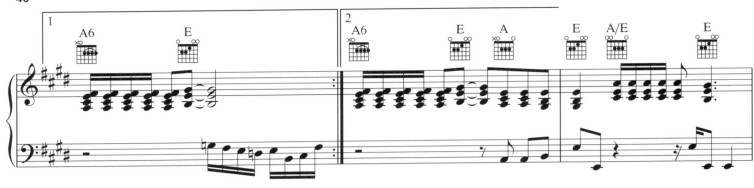

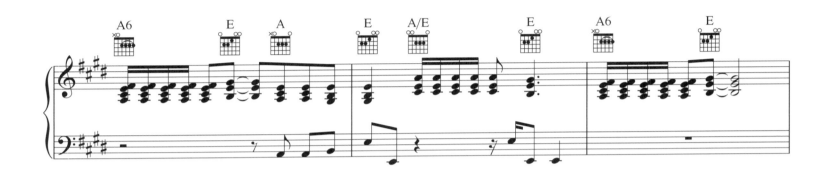

I am tired _ of this dev - il, I am tired _ of this stuff.

I am tired _ of this bus' - ness, so, _____ when the go-ing gets rough,

BLACK VELVET

Words and Music by DAVID TYSON
and CHRISTOPHER WARD

Moderately slow bluesy Shuffle

Mis-sis-sip-pi in the mid-dle of a dry __ spell. Jim-mie Rod - gers on the
Up in Mem-phis the mu-sic's like a heat wave. "White Light - nin'"

slow south-ern style.

A new re-li-gion _ that'll bring you _ to your knees.

Black vel - vet, _ if you please.

Black vel - vet, _ if you

please.

Ev-'ry word _ of ev-'ry song _

Black vel - vet, if __ you __ please. __

If you please. __

If __ you please. __

If you please.

Mm. _____ Mm. _____

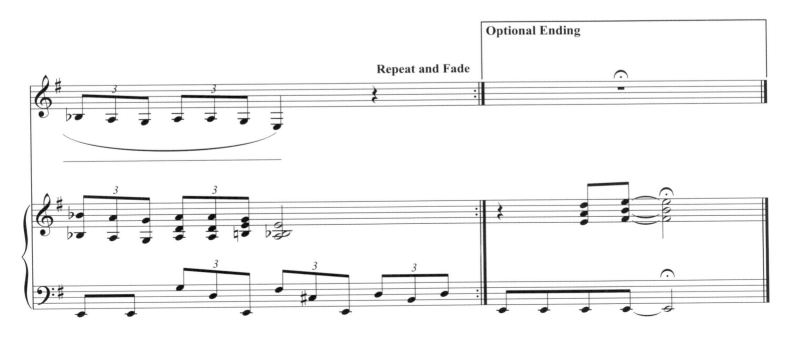

Repeat and Fade **Optional Ending**

THE BOY IS MINE

Words and Music by LaSHAWN DANIELS,
JAPHE TEJEDA, RODNEY JERKINS,
FRED JERKINS and BRANDY NORWOOD

Brandy: Excuse me, can I please talk to you for a minute?   *Monica:* Uh huh, sure. You know,

you look kind of familiar.   *Brandy:* Yeah, you do too. But, um, I just wanted to know, do you know

CANDLE IN THE WIND 1997

Words and Music by ELTON JOHN
and BERNIE TAUPIN

BRICK

Words and Music by BEN FOLDS
and DARREN JESSEE

BUTTERFLY KISSES

Words and Music by BOB CARLISLE
and RANDY THOMAS

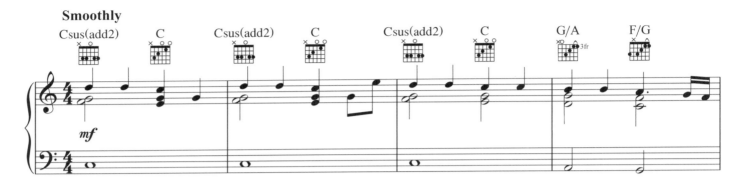

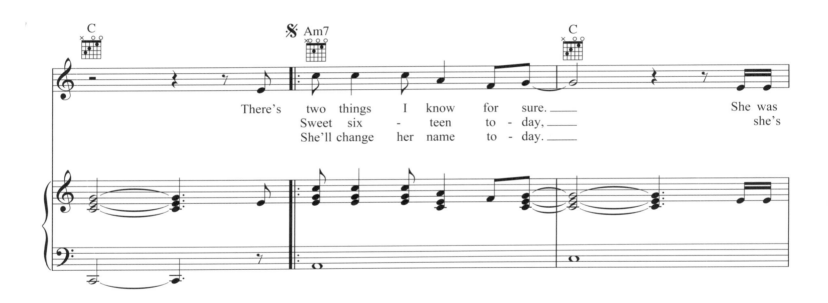

There's two things I know for sure. ___ She was
Sweet six - teen to - day, ___ she's
She'll change her name to - day. ___

sent here from heav - en, and she's dad - dy's lit - tle girl. ___ As I
look - ing like her mom - ma a lit - tle more ev - 'ry day. ___
She'll make a prom - ise, and I'll give her ___ a - way. ___

drop to my knees ___ by her bed ___ at night, ___
One part wom - an, the oth - er part girl. To
Stand - ing in the bride room just star - ing at her, she

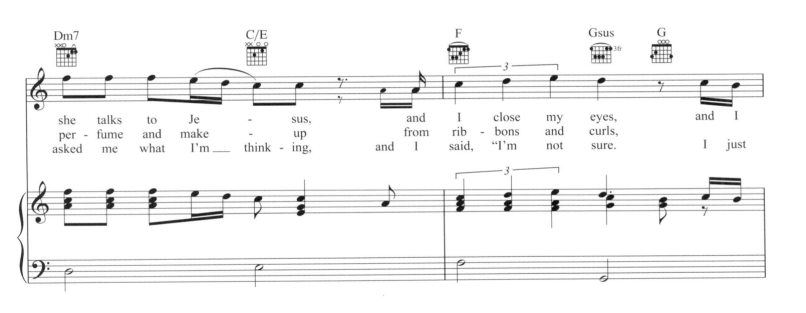

she talks to Je - sus, and I close my eyes, and I
per - fume and make - up from rib - bons and curls, and I
asked me what I'm ___ think - ing, and I said, "I'm not sure. I just

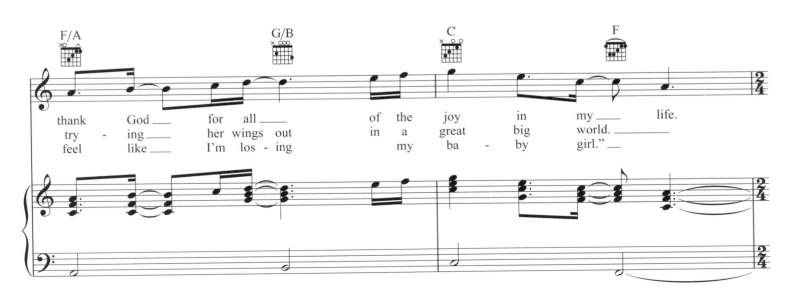

thank God ___ for all ___ of the joy in my ___ life.
try - ing ___ her wings out in a great big world. ___
feel like ___ I'm los - ing my ba - by girl." ___

Can You Feel The Love Tonight

from Walt Disney Pictures' THE LION KING

Music by ELTON JOHN
Lyrics by TIM RICE

CHANGE THE WORLD

Words and Music by WAYNE KIRKPATRICK,
GORDON KENNEDY and TOMMY SIMS

CRYIN'

Words and Music by
TYLER/PERRY/RHODES

There was a time _____ when I was so bro- ken-heart- ed.
It's down on me. _____ Yeah, I got to tell you one thing.

Love was- n't much _____ of a friend of mine.
It's been on my mind. _____ Girl, I got- ta say: _____

A
E
F♯m
D
cry - in' when I met you. Now I'm try - in' to for - get you.
A
E
D
Love is
Your love is
sweet mis - er - y.
A
E
I was cry - in' just to get you. Now I'm
C♯m
4fr
D
A
dy - in' 'cause I let you do what you

DON'T SPEAK

Words and Music by ERIC STEFANI
and GWEN STEFANI

DREAMS

Lyrics by DOLORES O'RIORDAN
Music by DOLORES O'RIORDAN
and NOEL HOGAN

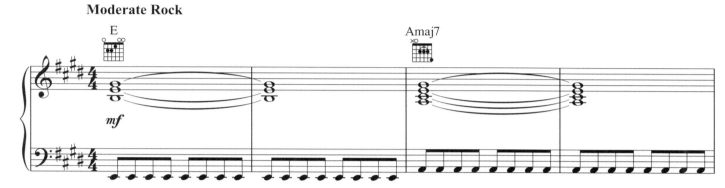

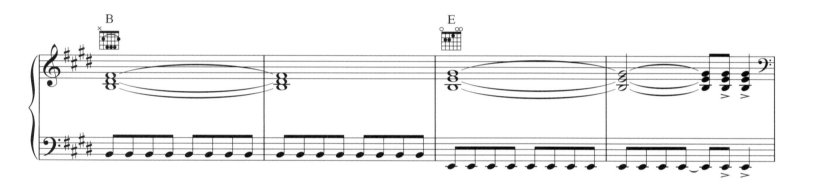

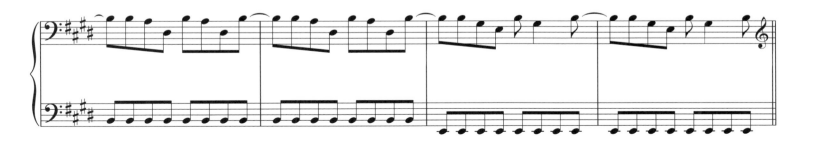

Repeat and Fade

(Everything I Do)
I DO IT FOR YOU

Words and Music by BRYAN ADAMS,
R.J. LANGE and MICHAEL KAMEN

EXHALE
(Shoop Shoop)

Words and Music by
BABYFACE

Easy R&B Ballad

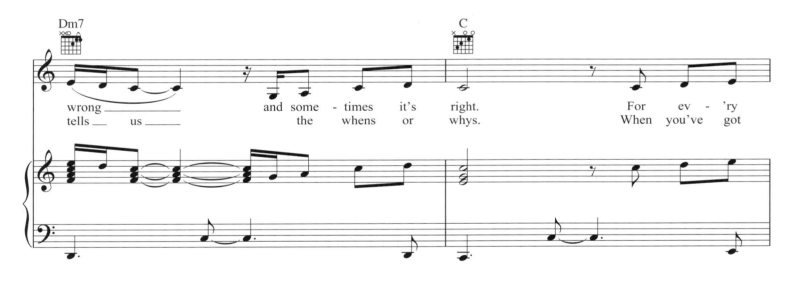

(1.) Ev - 'ry - one falls in love some - times. _____ Some - times it's
(2., 3.) laugh, some - times you'll cry. _____ Life nev - er

wrong _____ and some - times it's right. For ev - 'ry
tells _____ us _____ the whens or whys. When you've got

win some - one must fail, but there comes a
friends to wish you well, you'll find a

FIELDS OF GOLD

Music and Lyrics by
STING

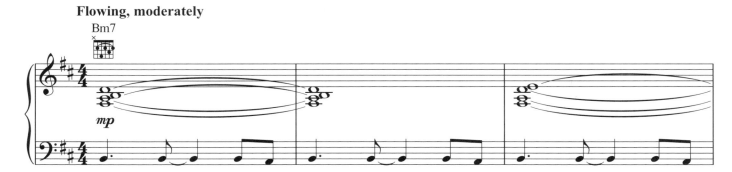

Man - y years have passed since those _
mem - ber me when the _

_ sum - mer days a - mong the fields _ of bar - ley. See the
_ west wind moves up - on the fields _ of bar - ley. You can

THE FRESHMEN

Words and Music by
BRIAN VANDER ARK

When I was young, I knew ev -
friend took a week's va -
We tried to wash our hands of

'ry - thing.
ca - tion to for - get her. His girl took a week's worth of Val - ium and slept. And now he's
all of this. We nev - er talk of a lack in re - la - tion - ships and how we're

E(add9)   A5   C#m

guilt - strick - en, sob-bing with my   head   on the floor.   Stop a ba - by's breath   and a
guilt - strick - en, sob-bing with his   head   on the floor.   Thinks __ a - bout her now and how he
guilt - strick - en, sob-bing with our   heads   on the floor.   We fell through the ice   when we

A   C#m   B   A

shoe - ful of rice, __ now.
nev - er real - ly wept. He says
tried   not to slip. We'd say
                                        I can't be held re - spon - si - ble, __

C#m   B   A   C#m   B

                        'cause she was touch-ing her face.   I

A   C#m   B   A   **To Coda** ⊕

won't be held re - spon - si - ble. __   She fell in love in the first place.

FRIENDS IN LOW PLACES

Words and Music by DeWAYNE BLACKWELL
and EARL BUD LEE

Moderately, with a beat

Blame it all on my roots. ___ I
guess I was wrong. ___ I

showed up in boots ___ and ru-ined your black-tie af-fair.
just don't be-long, ___ but then I've been there be-fore. ___

___ The last one to know; ___ the
___ Ev-'ry-thing's ___ all right. ___ I'll

FROM A DISTANCE

Words and Music by
JULIE GOLD

GENIE IN A BOTTLE

Words and Music by STEVE KIPNER,
DAVID FRANK and PAMELA SHEYNE

THE GIFT

Words and Music by TOM DOUGLAS
and JIM BRICKMAN

I FINALLY FOUND SOMEONE

Words and Music by BARBRA STREISAND,
MARVIN HAMLISCH, R.J. LANGE
and BRYAN ADAMS

Male: I fi-n'lly found some-one who knocks me off my feet.

I fi-n'lly found the one ___ that makes me feel com - plete.

Female: It start-ed o - ver cof - fee. We start-ed out as friends.

GOOD RIDDANCE
(Time of Your Life)

Words by BILLIE JOE
Music by GREEN DAY

An - oth - er turn - ing point, __ a fork __ stuck in __ the __ road.
So take the pho - to - graphs __ and still - frames in __ your __ mind.
Instrumental solo ad lib.

HARD TO SAY I'M SORRY

Words and Music by PETER CETERA
and DAVID FOSTER

HERE AND NOW

Words and Music by TERRY STEELE
and DAVID ELLIOT

HERO

Words and Music by MARIAH CAREY
and WALTER AFANASIEFF

Lyrics:

There's a he-ro if you look in-side ___ your heart. You don't
long ___ road when you face the world ___ a-lone. No one

have to be ___ a-fraid of what you are. There's an an-
reach-es out ___ a hand for you to hold. ___ You can find ___

-swer if you reach in-to ___ your soul and the
___ love if you search with-in ___ your-self ___ and the

HOW AM I SUPPOSED TO LIVE WITHOUT YOU

Words and Music by MICHAEL BOLTON
and DOUG JAMES

I DON'T WANT TO WAIT

Words and Music by
PAULA COLE

Strongly

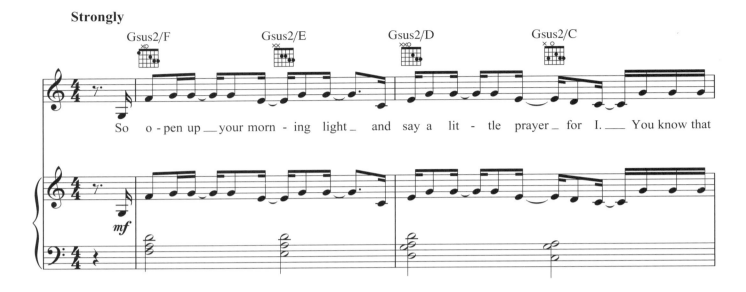

So o-pen up your morn-ing light and say a lit-tle prayer for I. You know that

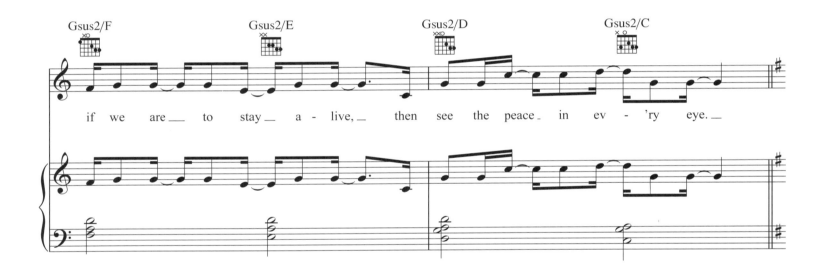

if we are to stay a-live, then see the peace in ev-'ry eye.

Du du du du du, du du du du du,

Repeat and Fade

I NEED TO KNOW

Moderately, not too fast

Words and Music by CORY ROONEY
and MARC ANTHONY

They say a - round ___ the way ___ you've asked ___
My ev - 'ry thought ___ is of ___ this be -
La gen - te an - da ___ di - cien - do por ___
Si yo pu - die - ra a ca - ri - ciar ___

I SWEAR

Words and Music by FRANK MYERS
and GARY BAKER

I see the ques - tions in ___ your eyes; ___ I know what's weigh -
I'll give you ev - 'ry - thing _ I can; ___ I'll build your dreams _

I WANT IT THAT WAY

Words and Music by MAX MARTIN
and ANDREAS CARLSSON

I WILL ALWAYS LOVE YOU

Words and Music by
DOLLY PARTON

will_ al - ways_ love_ you. _____ I _____

D.S.

will_ al - ways_ love_ you. _____

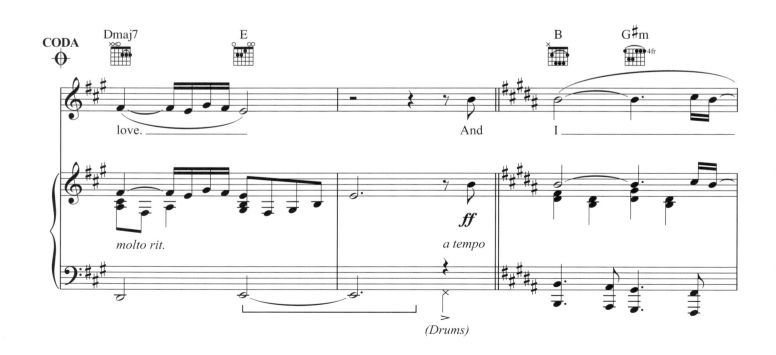

CODA

love. _____ And _____ I _____

molto rit.   a tempo

(Drums)

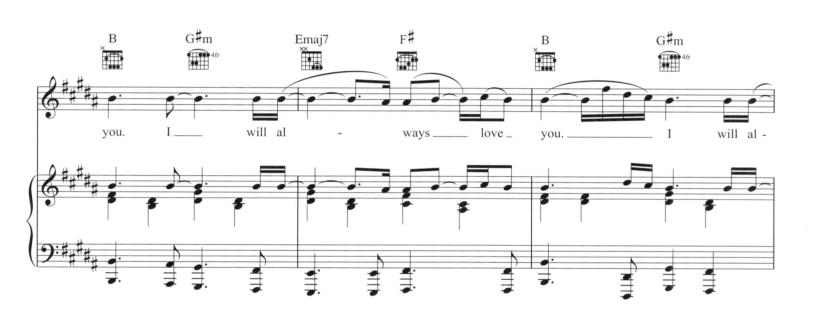

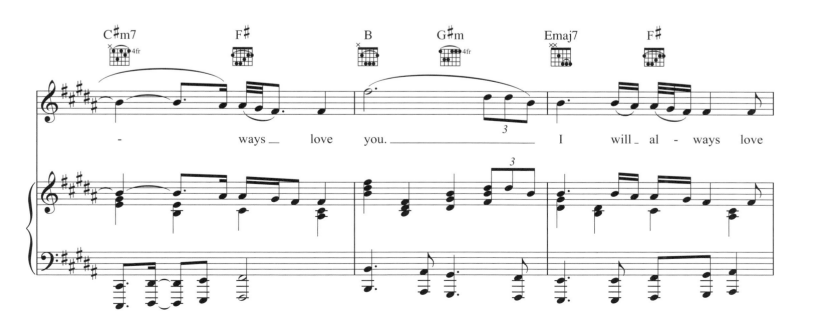

Additional Lyrics

3. I hope life treats you kind.
   And I hope you have all you've dreamed of.
   And I wish to you, joy and happiness.
   But above all this, I wish you love.

I WILL REMEMBER YOU

Theme from THE BROTHERS McMULLEN

Words and Music by SARAH McLACHLAN,
SEAMUS EGAN and DAVE MERENDA

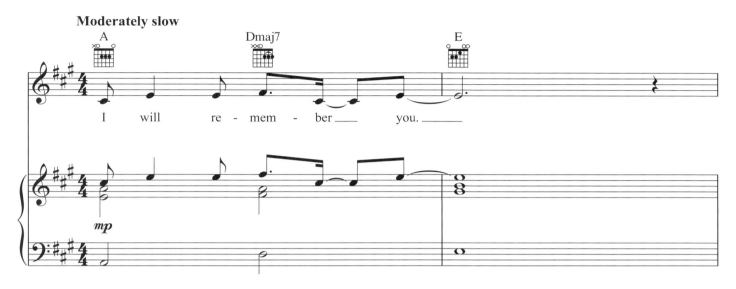

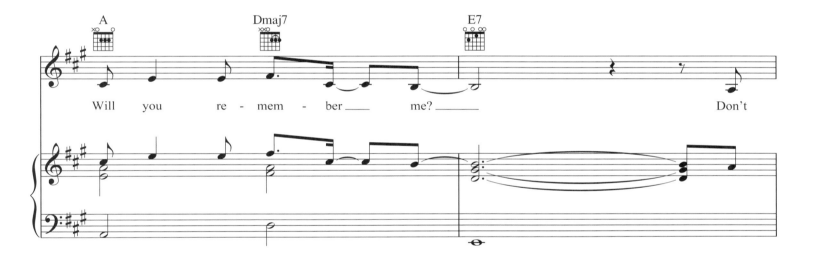

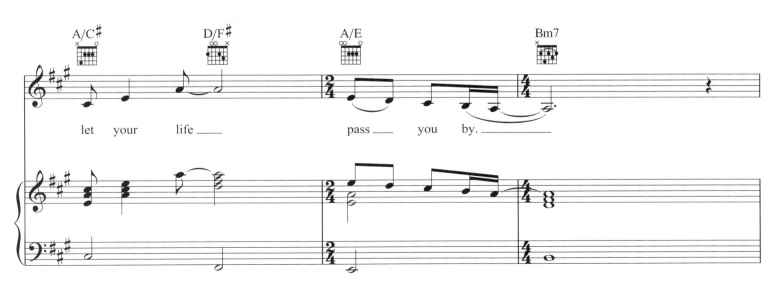

I'LL MAKE LOVE TO YOU

Words and Music by
BABYFACE

IF YOU HAD MY LOVE

Words and Music by RODNEY JERKINS,
LaSHAWN DANIELS, CORY ROONEY,
FRED JERKINS and JENNIFER LOPEZ

Bm

you had my love and I gave ___ you all my trust, would you com -

Em7 · F#m7

- fort ___ me?   { Tell ___ me, ba - by. }   And if ___

Bm

___ some - how you knew that your love ___ would be un - true, would you lie ___

Em7 · F#m7

___ to ___ me and call me ___ "ba - by"?   { Now if I give ___ you
                                                You said you want ___ my

I'M THE ONLY ONE

Words and Music by
MELISSA ETHERIDGE

Steady Rock

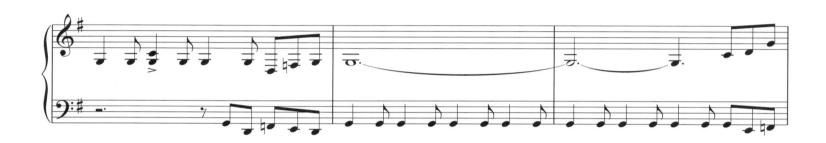

Please, baby, can't_ you see my
Please, baby, can't_ you see I'm

mind's a burn-in' hell. _ I got ra-zors a-rip-pin' and tear-in' and strip-in' my
try-in' to ex-plain. _ I've been here be-fore and I'm lock-in' the door and I'm

IF I EVER LOSE MY FAITH IN YOU

Music and Lyrics by
STING

IRONIC

Lyrics by ALANIS MORISSETTE
Music by ALANIS MORISSETTE
and GLEN BALLARD

G/B Am7 G/B C(add2)
think? A lit - tle too i - ron - ic... and yeah, I
G/B Am7 G C
real - ly do think... it's like rain on your
G Am7 G C
wed - ding day. It's a free ride when you've
G Am7 G C
al - read - y paid. It's the good ad - vice that you

JUMP, JIVE AN' WAIL

Words and Music by
LOUIS PRIMA

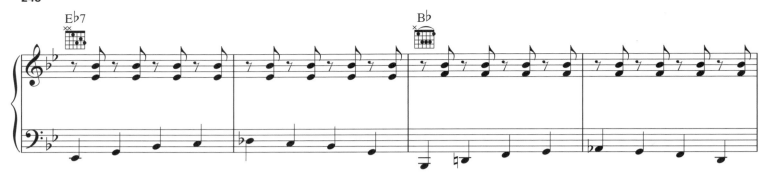

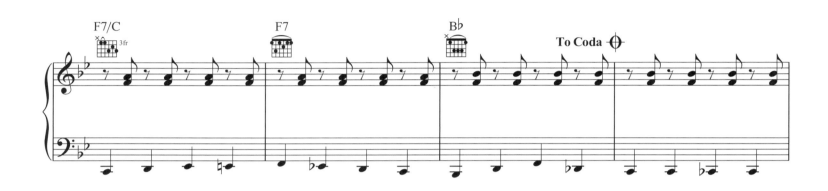

Pa-pa's in the ice-box look-ing for a _____ can of ale.

Pa-pa's in the ice-box look-ing for a _____ can of ale.

LIVIN' LA VIDA LOCA

Words and Music by DESMOND CHILD
and ROBI ROSA

Fast, with a steady beat

She's in-to su-per-sti - tions, black cats and voo-doo dolls. __ I feel a prem-o-ni - tion. That girl's gon-na make me fall. __

KISS FROM A ROSE

Words and Music by
SEAL

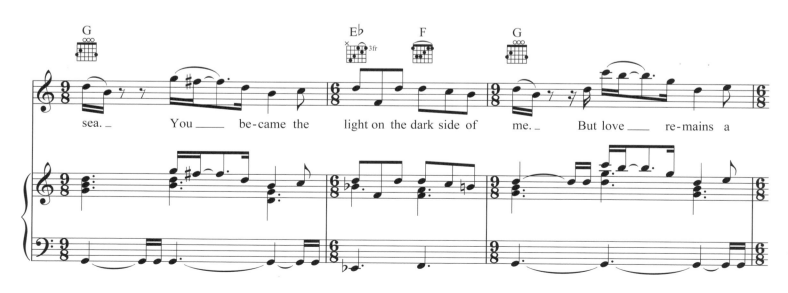

LOSER

Words by BECK HANSEN
Music by BECK HANSEN and KARL STEPHENSON

To Coda

los - er, ba - by. _____ So, why don't you kill me? _____

Rap 2: *(See rap lyrics)*

Soy un per-di-dor. I'm a

los-er, ba-by. So, why don't you kill me?

D5

Rap Lyrics

Rap 1: In the time of chimpanzees, I was a monkey.
Butane in my veins and a mouth to cut the junkies with the plastic eyeballs.
Spray paint the vegetables. Dog food skulls with the beefcake pantyhose.
Kill the headlights and put it in neutral.
Got a couple of couches Stockcar flaming with the loser and the cruise control.
Baby's in Reno with the vitamin D. Got a couple of couches
Asleep on the love seat.
Someone keeps saying I'm insane to complain about a shotgun wedding
And a stain on my shirt.
Don't believe everything that you breathe.
You get a parking violation and a maggot on your sleeve.
So shave your face with some mace in the dark
Saving all your food stamps and burning down the trailer park.
Bent all the music with the phony gas chamber.
Yo, cut it.
Chorus

Rap 2: Forces of evil and a bozo nightmare.
'Cause one's got a weasel and another's got a flag.
One's on the pole. Shove the other in a bag with the rerun shows
And the cocaine nose job, the daytime crap of the folk singer slob.
He hung himself with guitar string.
A slab of turkey neck and it's hangin' from a pigeon wing.
So get right if you can't relate. Trade the cash for the beef
For the body for the hate.
And my time is a piece of wax falling on a termite
Who's choking on the splinters.
Chorus

MACARENA

Words and Music by ANTONIO ROMERO
and RAFAEL RUIZ

boy whose name _ is Ni-co-ri-no. I don't want him, could-n't stand him!

(Spoken:) He was no good, so I... *(laughs)* *Oh, come on,*

what was I supposed to do? *He was out of town, and his two friends were so fine!*

Da-le a tu cuer-po a-le-gri-a, Ma-ca-re-na. Que tu cuer-po es pa' dar-le a-le-gri-a y co-sa bue-na.

LOSING MY RELIGION

Words and Music by WILLIAM BERRY,
PETER BUCK, MICHAEL MILLS
and MICHAEL STIPE

(Can't Live Without Your)
LOVE AND AFFECTION

Words and Music by MARC TANNER,
MATT NELSON and GUNNAR NELSON

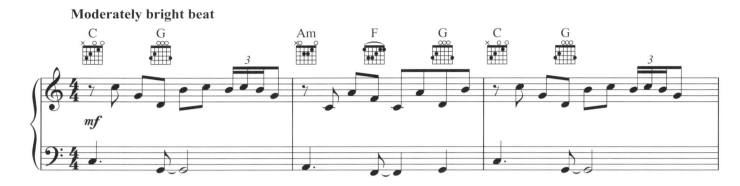

Here _____ she comes,
goes.
wait,

mm, _____
No,
mm, _____

_____ she just like an an - gel. _____ Seems like for - ev - er that she's
she don't know what she's miss - ing. Can't _____ she see I'll nev - er
here for an an - swer. _____ Won - der if to - mor - row will be

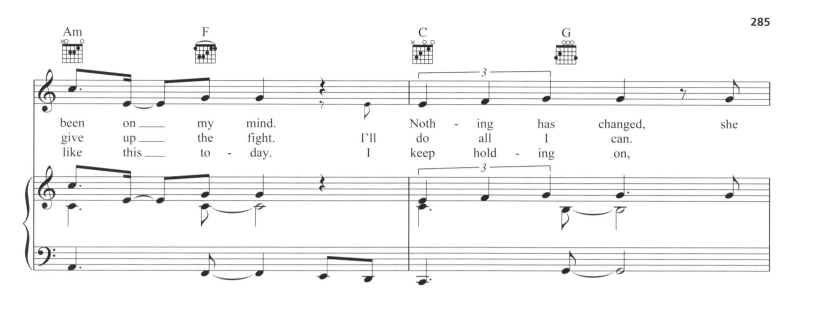

been on ____ my mind.
give up ____ the fight.
like this ____ to - day.

Noth - ing has changed, she
I'll do all I can.
I keep hold - ing on,

thinks I'm a waste of her time. _____
She un - der - stands my de -
can't go on liv - ing this

There __ she

sire. _____
way, _____

ba - by. _____

I've been on the out -
I've been on the out -

love.

With your love, _____ I put my arms a - round _ you.

MISSING

Words by TRACEY THORN
Music by BEN WATT

Moderate Dance tempo

Lyrics:

I step off __ the train. __ I'm
Could you __ be dead? __ You

walk-ing down __ your street __ a - gain and past __ your __ door,
al - ways were __ two steps __ a - head of __ ev - 'ry - one.

__ but you don't live __ there an - y - more. ____ It's
__ We'd walk be - hind __ while you would run. ____ I

MMM BOP

Words and Music by ISAAC HANSON,
TAYLOR HANSON and ZAC HANSON

NO RAIN

Words and Music by
BLIND MELON

MORE THAN WORDS

Words and Music by NUNO BETTENCOURT
and GARY CHERONE

Say-in' "I _____ love _____ you" is
Now that I've _____ tried _____ to

not the words _ I _____ want _____ to _____ hear _____ from _____ you. _____ It's not that I _____
talk to you _____ and make _____ you _____ un - der - stand, _____ all _____ you _____

MY HEART WILL GO ON
(Love Theme from 'Titanic')
from the Paramount and Twentieth Century Fox Motion Picture TITANIC

Music by JAMES HORNER
Lyric by WILL JENNINGS

ONE

Lyrics by BONO and THE EDGE
Music by U2

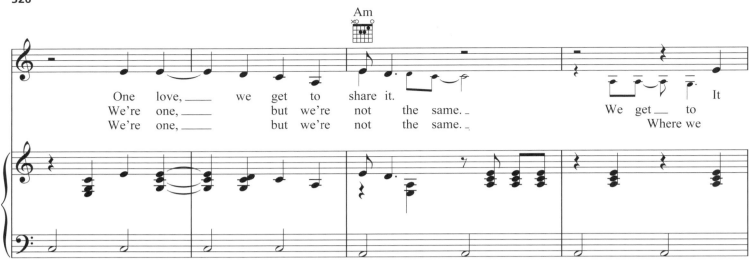

One love, _____ we get to share it.
We're one, _____ but we're not the same. _____
We're one, _____ but we're not the same. _____

We get ___ to
Where we

leaves you, ba - by, if you don't care for it. _____
car - ry each oth - er, car - ry each oth - er.
hurt each oth - er, and we're do - in' it a - gain.

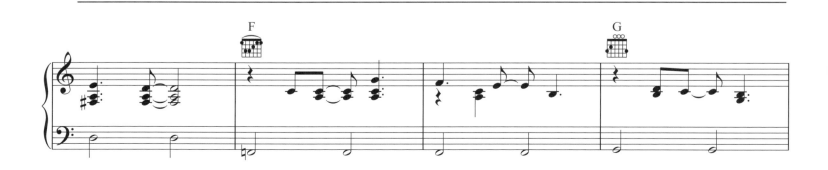

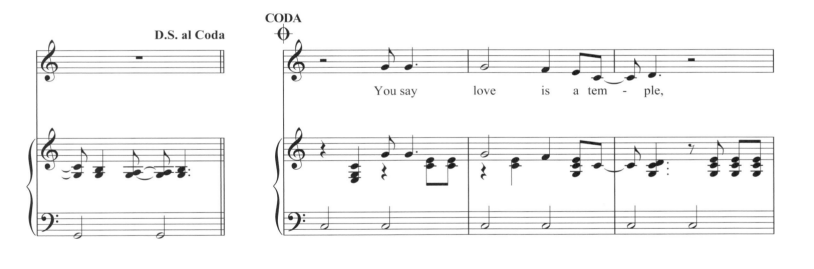

You say love is a tem - ple,

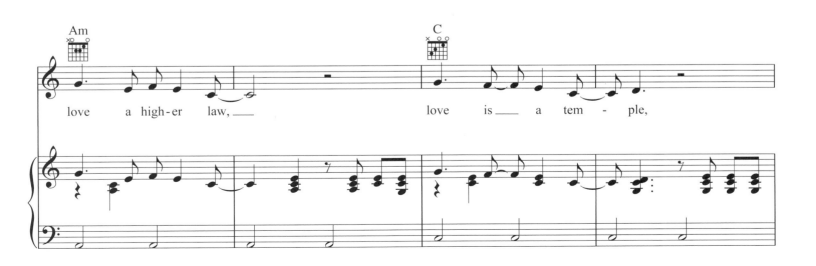

love a high-er law, ___ love is ___ a tem - ple,

RIGHT HERE, RIGHT NOW

Words and Music by
JESUS JONES

ONLY WANNA BE WITH YOU

Words and Music by DARIUS CARLOS RUCKER,
EVERETT DEAN FELBER, MARK WILLIAM BRYAN
and JAMES GEORGE SONEFELD

You and me, ___ we come from dif-f'rent worlds. _

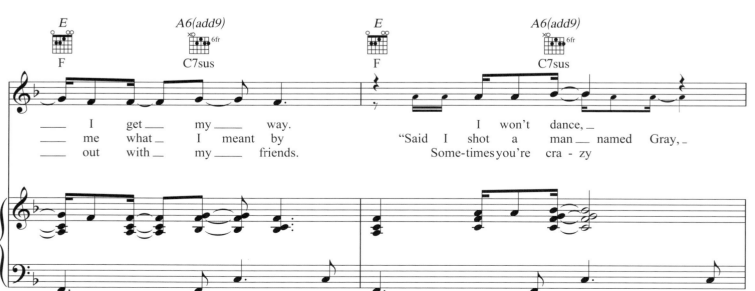

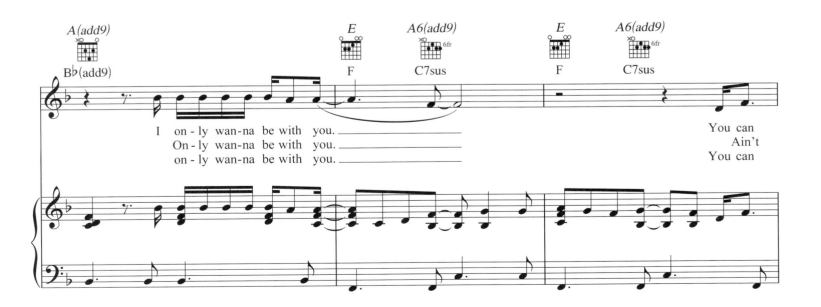

THE POWER OF LOVE

Words by MARY SUSAN APPLEGATE and JENNIFER RUSH
Music by CANDY DEROUGE and GUNTHER MENDE

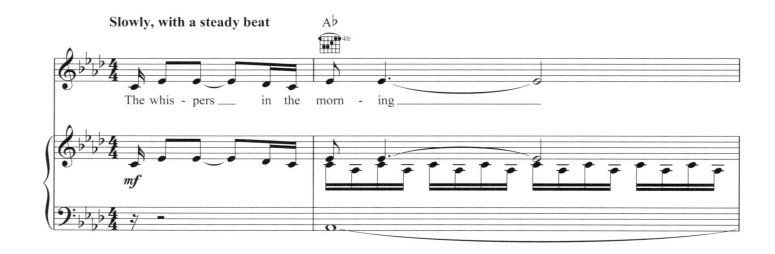

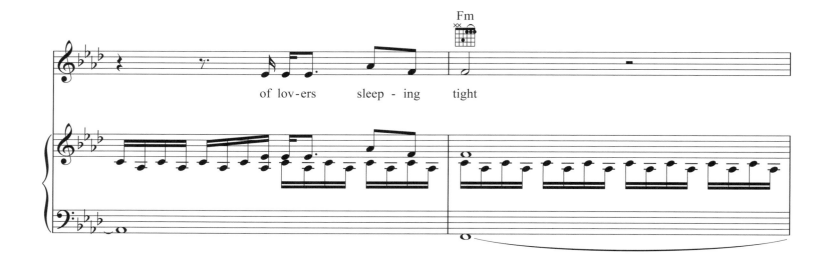

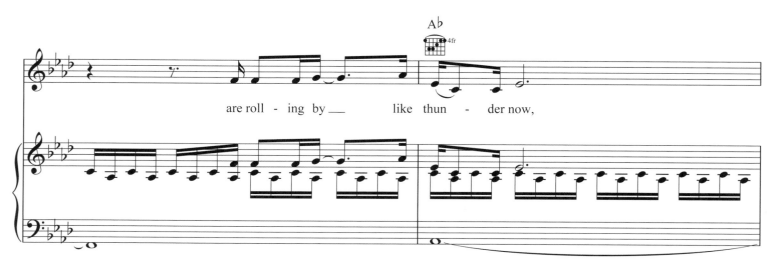

RUNAWAY TRAIN

Words and Music by
DAVID PIRNER

Call you up in the mid-dle of the night,   like a fi-re-fly with-
Can you help me re-mem-ber how to smile?   Make it some-how all

out a light. __   You were there like a blow-torch burn-ing.
seem worth-while. __   How on earth did I get so jad-ed?

I was a key that could use a lit-tle turn-ing __   So tired that I
Life's mys-ter-y seems so fad-ed. __   I can go where
                                                        (D.S.) Instrumental

Save the Best for Last

Words and Music by WENDY WALDMAN,
PHIL GALDSTON and JON LIND

SMELLS LIKE TEEN SPIRIT

Words and Music by KURT COBAIN,
KRIST NOVOSELIC and DAVE GROHL

Load up ___ on guns, ___ bring ___ your friends. ___
I'm worse ___ at what ___ I ___ do best, ___
And I ___ for - get ___ just why I ___ taste. ___

It's fun ___ to lose ___ and to ___ pre - tend. ___ She's o - ver - bored, ___
and for ___ this gift ___ I feel ___ blessed. ___ Our lit - tle trap ___
Oh, yeah, ___ I guess ___ it makes ___ me smile. ___ I found ___ it hard; ___

SMOOTH

Words by ROB THOMAS
Music by ROB THOMAS and ITAAL SHUR

SOMETHING TO TALK ABOUT
(Let's Give Them Something to Talk About)

Words and Music by
SHIRLEY EIKHARD

Moderate Reggae/Rock

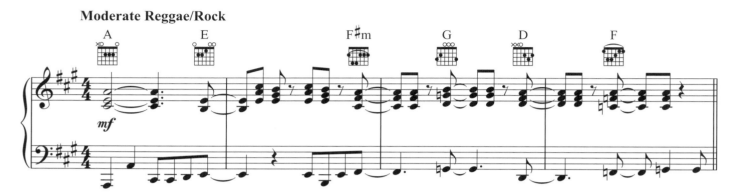

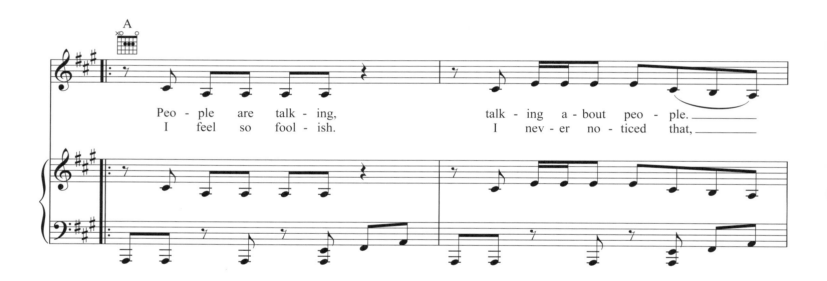

Peo - ple are talk - ing, talk - ing a - bout peo - ple. _____
I feel so fool - ish. I nev - er no - ticed that, _____

I hear them whis - per, you won't _ be - lieve it.
ba - by, you're act - ing so nerv - ous, like _____ you're fall - ing.

Let's give them some-thing to talk a - bout.
Come on, give them some-thing to talk a - bout,

Let's give them _ some-thing to
a lit - tle _ mys - t'ry to

talk a - bout. ___
fig - ure out. ___

I wan-na give them some-thing to talk a - bout. I want your love. _

And ___

TEARS IN HEAVEN

Words and Music by ERIC CLAPTON
and WILL JENNINGS

Be-yond the door ___ there's peace, I'm sure, ___

and I know ___ there'll be no more ___ tears in heav -

en.

D.S. al Coda

CODA

en.

rall.

STRONG ENOUGH

Words and Music by KEVIN GILBERT,
DAVID BAERWALD, SHERYL CROW,
BRIAN McLEOD, BILL BOTTRELL
and DAVID RICKETTS

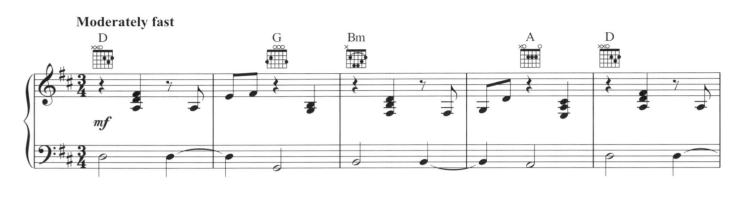

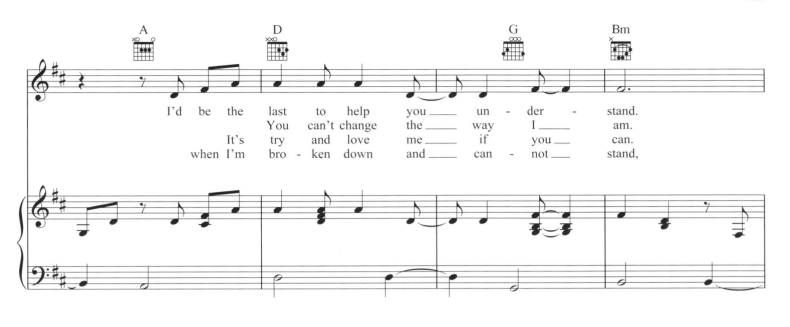

I'd be the last to help you ___ un - der - stand.
You can't change the ___ way I ___ am.
It's try and love me ___ if you ___ can.
when I'm bro - ken down and ___ can - not ___ stand,

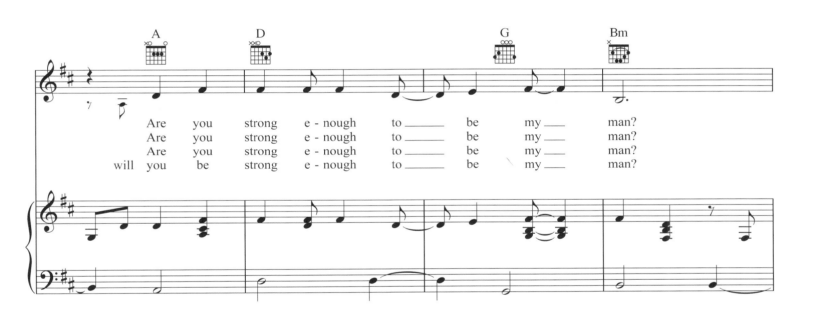

Are you strong e - nough to ___ be my ___ man?
Are you strong e - nough to ___ be my ___ man?
Are you strong e - nough to ___ be my ___ man?
will you be strong e - nough to ___ be my ___ man?

My ___ man.
My ___ man.

but please, _____ don't leave. _____

leave. _____

TO BE WITH YOU

Words and Music by ERIC MARTIN
and DAVID GRAHAME

I'm the one who wants to be with you. _____ Deep in-side I hope you'll

feel _____ it, too. _____ Wait-ed on a line _____ of

greens and blues _____ just to be the next to

be _____ with you. _____ I'm the one who wants to

UN-BREAK MY HEART

Words and Music by
DIANE WARREN

Don't leave me in ___ all this pain. ___ Don't leave me out ___ in the rain. ___
Take back that sad ___ word, "good - bye." ___ Bring back the joy ___ to my life. ___

UNDER THE BRIDGE

Words and Music by ANTHONY KIEDIS,
FLEA, JOHN FRUSCIANTE
and CHAD SMITH

Slow Rock Ballad

Some-times I feel ____ like I
drive on her streets ____ 'cause
hard to be-lieve ____ that there's

don't have a part ― ner.
she's my com-pan ― ion. I
no-bod-y out ____ there It's

Some-times I feel ____ like
walk through her hills 'cause she
hard to be-lieve ____ that

VISION OF LOVE

Words and Music by MARIAH CAREY
and BEN MARGULIES

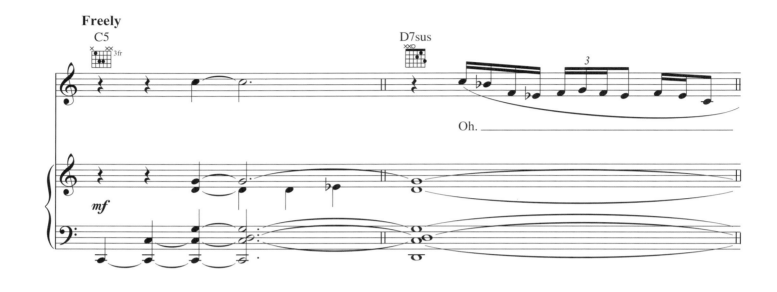

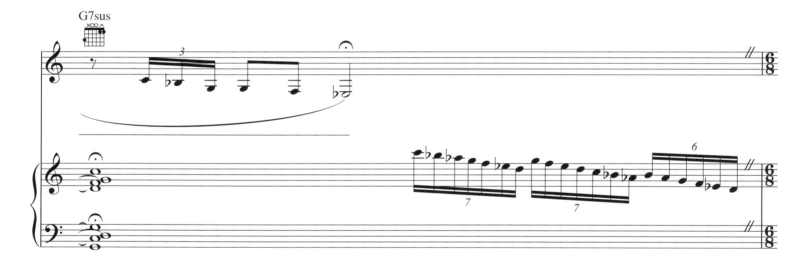

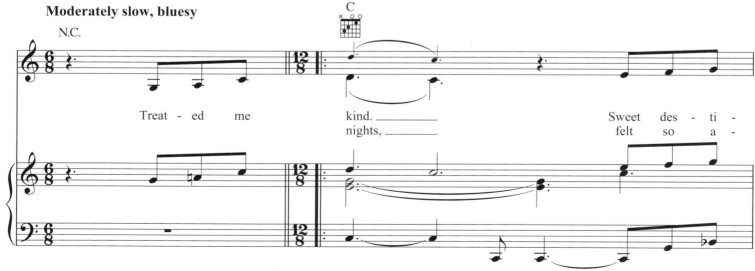

WANNABE

Words and Music by GERI HALLIWELL,
EMMA BUNTON, MELANIE BROWN,
MELANIE CHISHOLM, VICTORIA ADAMS,
and MATTHEW ROWEBOTTOM

WHAT'S UP

Words and Music by
LINDA PERRY

Twen-ty-five years of my life and still __ I'm trying to get up that
And I try, oh my God, do I try, I

great big hill __ of hope
try all the time

for a des-ti-na-
in this in-sti-tu-

ooh, _____ uh - huh.

rit.

Slower, easy Shuffle (♪♪ = ♪♪)

Twen-ty-five years of my

life and still ___ I'm trying to get up that great big hill __ of hope _

for a des - ti - na - tion.

rit.

WHEN YOU SAY NOTHING AT ALL

Words and Music by DON SCHLITZ
and PAUL OVERSTREET

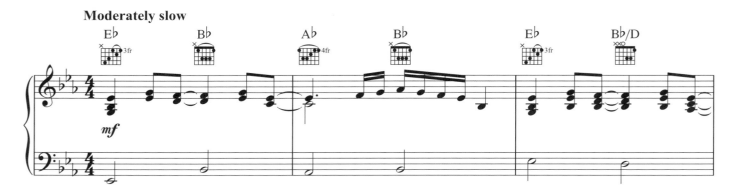

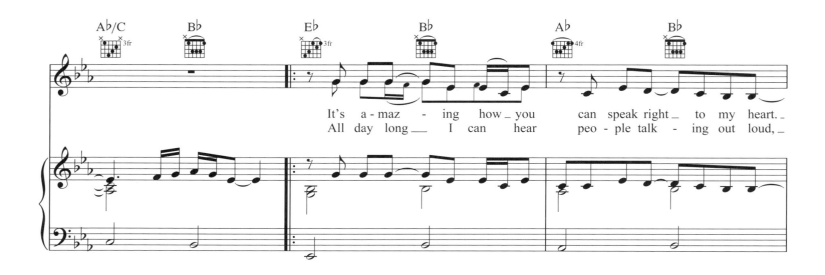

It's a - maz - ing how _ you can speak right _ to my heart.
All day long _ I can hear peo - ple talk - ing out loud, _

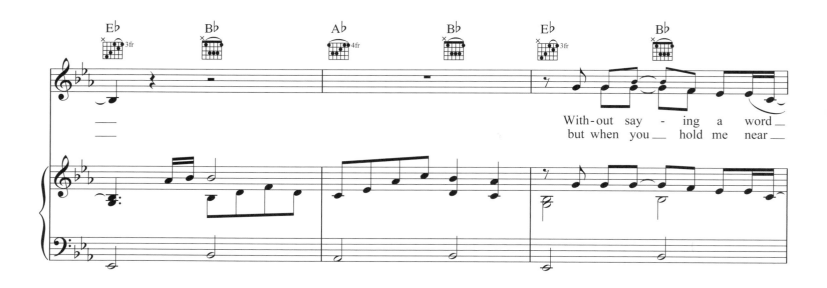

With - out say - ing a word _
but when you _ hold me near _

truth in your eyes _____ say - ing you'll _____ nev - er leave _____ me. A

touch of your hand _____ says you'll catch _____ me if ev - er I fall. _____

Now you say it best _____ when you say noth - ing at all. _

A WHOLE NEW WORLD

from Disney ALADDIN

Music by ALAN MENKEN
Lyrics by TIM RICE

Sweetly

I can show _ you the world,

shin - ing, shim - mer - ing, splen - did. Tell me, prin - cess, now

when did you last let your heart _ de - cide? _

WONDERWALL

Words and Music by
NOEL GALLAGHER

you're gon - na be the one that saves me, _____ and af - ter all, _

you're my won - der - wall. _____

I said may - be _____

you're gon - na be the one that saves me, _____ and af - ter all, _

YOU MUST LOVE ME

from the Cinergi Motion Picture EVITA

Words by TIM RICE
Music by ANDREW LLOYD WEBBER

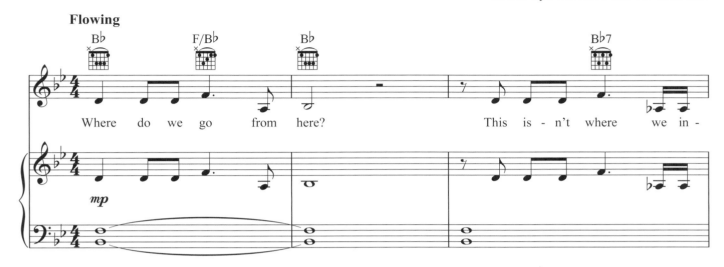

Flowing

Where do we go from here? This is-n't where we in-

tend-ed to be. __ We had it all, __ you be-lieved __ in me, __ I be-

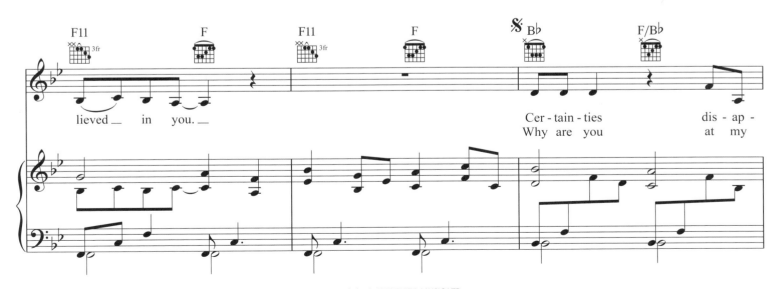

lieved __ in you. __

Cer-tain-ties   dis-ap-
Why are you   at my

You Were Meant For Me

Words and Music by JEWEL MURRAY
and STEVE POLTZ

I hear the clock. It's six A. M.
I called my ma-ma, she was out for a walk. Con-
I brush my teeth, I put the cap back on.

I feel so far from where I've been.
soled a cup of cof-fee, but it did-n't want to talk. So, I
I know you hate it when I leave the light on. I

I got my eggs. I got my
picked up the pa-per, it was
pick up a cup and then I

pan - cakes, too. _____ I got my ma-ple syr-up, ev-'ry-thing but _____ you. _____
more bad news. _____ My heart's be-ing bro-ken by peo-ple be-ing used. _____
turn the sheets down _____ and then I take a deep breath, a good look _____ a - round. _____

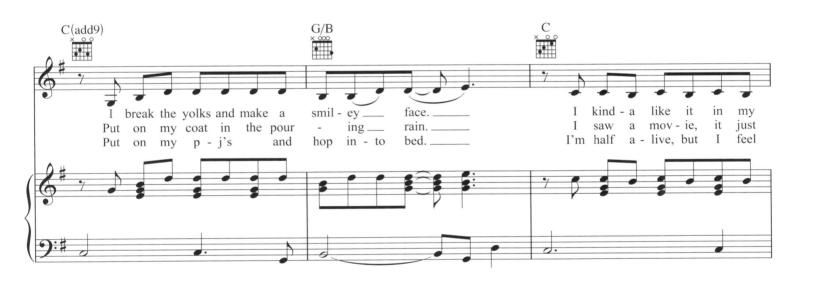

I break the yolks and make a smil - ey _____ face. _____ I kind-a like it in my
Put on my coat in the pour - ing _____ rain. _____ I saw a mov - ie, it just
Put on my p - j's and hop in - to bed. _____ I'm half a - live, but I feel

brand-new place. _____ I wipe the spots up off the mirror, don't leave my keys in the door. _____ I
was-n't the same 'cause it was hap - py or I was sad, _____ and
most-ly dead. I try and tell my-self it - 'll be all _____ right. _____

YOU'LL BE IN MY HEART

(Pop Version)

from Walt Disney Pictures' TARZAN™

Words and Music by
PHIL COLLINS

Moderately

Come stop your cry - ing; _ it will be all right. Just take my hand,

hold it tight. _____ I will pro-tect you from all a - round _ you.

I will be here; don't you _ cry.

For one so small you

Why can't they un - der-stand the

YOU'RE STILL THE ONE

Words and Music by SHANIA TWAIN
and R.J. LANGE

YOU'VE GOT A FRIEND IN ME

from Walt Disney's TOY STORY

Music and Lyrics by
RANDY NEWMAN